THE SECRET PRINCIPLES OF FEMALE POWERS

I0425249

BY
JEFF UNAEGBU
&
EMMANUEL IBUOT

"How many more wills will Habit deceive?
Fettered and guillotined, souls rest in tears.
How endless lost souls dreamily receive
Death's melody, not Admonition's fears!"
         ___ Anonymous

First published 2009 by Global Publishers,
Nsukka, Enugu State.
Published 2019 by FIRM Publishers,
Cine Unit, Institute of African Studies, University of Nigeria,
Nsukka.

© Jeff Unaegbu and Emmanuel Ibuot, 2009, 2019.

ISBN: 9781087373515

National Library of Nigeria Cataloguing in Publication Data:
Unaegbu, Jeff; Ibuot Emmanuel
The Secret Principles of Female Powers
        I.   Nigerian Non-fiction (English)
        II.   Title
All correspondences to
   (1)   The authors via (a) +2348035272576,
                    (b) +2348064153497

Set on 11 pts Franklin Gothic Medium
MADE IN NIGERIA

DEDICATION

TO GOD ALMIGHTY FOR
CREATING
THE MALE AND THE FEMALE,
ADAM AND EVE,
YIN AND YANG....

ACKNOWLEDGEMENT
We are grateful to the following people for their indefatigable support and sincere goodwill for our welfare in this life: Mr. and Mrs. John Unaegbu and Mr. and Mrs. Ededet Cletus, our parents, and, Professor C.O. Nebo, Professor A.O.E. Animalu, Professor J.C.A. Agbakoba, and Rev. Fr. (Prof.) A.N. Akwanya, our mentors.

A SOBER NOTE TO THE READER:

Wow! Guess what? This book is indeed a masterpiece. These astute writers (Mr. Unaegbu and Mr. Ibuot) have, through this book, distinguished themselves in the pages of history. They have just as much, and in all honesty, unmasked the daunting issue of the unscriptural dominance of female powers over men in this world. I do recommend this book, *The Secret Principles of Female Powers,* to all the men and women out there who are having a hard time in striking the balance in their relationships, which is God's utmost idea. Read and be transformed....

- Pastor Wisdom A. Okoronkwo

TABLE OF CONTENTS

PRESCRIPT

Dear friend,

We undertook to do a work of this kind because of some very real yet subtle social phenomena. These phenomena are surprisingly unspoken. They are almost lost in an intricate web called the conspiracy of silence. Over the years, working individually, we gradually grew a conscious appreciation of them and we began to gather facts, mostly based on active observation. It is simply a protective secret but naturally cultivated system encircling all of the feminine gender of the human race. This universal system maintains itself by having no universal queen to superintend its proceedings, thereby cutting off the feminine weakness for territorial tussles in that universal scale. Every female is a queen in this system. And because of this, every female is subtly wary of other females. This is even found between a mother and her daughter. We call it a system because it has house rules. These house rules or secret principles define and maintain it. *These house rules are encoded in the feminine gene. Thus, they are instinctive.* The rules have always been the same even before Cleopatra, the seductress with a difference. What is this system all about? It exists only to protect women from the advances and dominion of men. And when men finally break through or "conquer" women with their advances, it enables women to remain in control, though without men having the slightest inkling of the situation at hand. It is simply a system designed thousands of years ago to protect all female members from being dominated by men. And there is no female who is not a member, however fiercely any female would deny knowledge of such a system. We have observed that every female grows and gains experience in the system. Therefore, there are those who are almost unconscious of all or some of the house rules, yet use them by intuition. There are those who are barely conscious of the house rules and there are those who are fully conscious of most or all of the house rules. Still, all females are queens who use their intuition and instinct in moments of desperation. The wonderful intuition of women makes them all automatically connected in the world wide web of the system. We have chosen to call this system "the secret principles of female powers". Yes, it is nothing away from being an order of principles. It is a secret one too due to its entanglement in the conspiracy of silence.

Recently, the authors surprisingly discovered that they have been silently gathering data independently on this same system without knowing it. This realization naturally popped up during a casual conversation. Instantly, we deliberated on the urgent need of making known the house rules we have gathered. We also understood that our dear female folks should be given a fair hearing on the issue. Besides, there was the need to diversify our research method from simply being solely dependent on participant observation to also being dependent on survey, using questionnaire as the tool of data collection. Thus, we designed a questionnaire and got females to vet the house rules we have gathered. We did this after carefully hiding our masculine identities so that we do not stir up the intuitive house rule of non-cooperation or deliberate error mongering. Why did we do all these? We wanted to make sure that we are not influenced into any parallax error arising from viewing from the "high" masculine observatory. We also wanted to dish out the house rules through a book, this book. We hope the book would either remind the world of or bring the attention of the world to the existence of this natural system and would help men make wiser decisions in the art of wooing ladies.

In anticipation of future critical reviews, may we submit, *ab initio*, that the house rules are not fixed but relative laws. They are very flexible and, like water, they can assume different states depending on cultural and socio-political environment and the individuality of the woman using them. Furthermore, we did not set out to make a great book that would contain *all* the house rules ever used. Therefore, the house rules we have exposed are actually the negligible, yet fundamental, part of the system of rules. We have also provided a strategy to each house rule. The strategies also display these same characteristics as the house rules. The house rules are in the first person plural to reflect their universality, especially as they are encoded in every female. The strategies are pieces of advice in the second person singular for males to use in this game of hide-and-seek.

There is a war going on, cold war. It has been prosecuted for thousands of years – in fact from the moment either an historical or symbolic Eve began to make her own decisions without the slightest regard for her hubby. It is the war of the sexes. We understand that we are exposing the state-of-the-art ancient and modern weaponry of the female. We understand that we are disclosing the result of years of espionage. Therefore, many females would regard this book with a righteous indignation. This is only natural and highly expected. However, if they understand that we are not trying to lay bare their weapons of war to spite them, but are trying to make the job of male-and-female relationships easier, more modern and balanced, less instinctively ancient and quicker, then we would have achieved our aim. For, friend, we are respectful gentlemen and also have beautiful women in our own personal lives that we love as dearly as they love us….

Sincerely yours,
Jeff Unaegbu and Emmanuel Ibuot,

3:25 a.m.,
December 16, 2008.
Nsukka,
Nigeria.

HOUSE RULE 1:

WE SUPPRESS ANY EMOTIONAL DISPLAY THAT WOULD GIVE US AWAY AS CONQUERED OR READY TO BE CONQUERED IN ORDER TO IMMEDIATELY DRAW THE SAME WEAK DISPLAY FROM THE MAN WHOSE PRIDE WE WANT TO BREAK OR WHO WE FEAR CAN CONQUER US.

****

STRATEGY 1:

WHEN YOU DO NOT GET AN EXPECTED EMOTIONAL DISPLAY OF SUBMISSION FROM US, BE ON GUARD. SUPPRESS YOUR OWN EMOTIONS. NATURE ABHORS VACUUM. NATURE WOULD TRY TO MAKE YOU GIVE THE SAME DISPLAY TO CANCEL THE DISEQUILIBRIUM. BE ON GUARD. WE WOULD BE FORCED TO BURST LIKE A DAM IF AND ONLY IF YOU HAVE NOT DIMINISHED YOUR CONTACTS WITH US.

HOUSE RULE 2:

WHILE WALKING TOGETHER, WE MOVE A FEW STEPS BEHIND THE MAN WE DO NOT WANT PEOPLE TO SEE AS OUR PARTNER IN LOVE OR IN FRIENDSHIP.

****

STRATEGY 2:

IF YOU ARE INTERESTED IN US AND WE ARE WALKING TOGETHER WITH YOU IN THAT MANNER, PRETEND NOT TO NOTICE OUR EVASION. DECIDE WHETHER TO DUMP US OR TO CONTINUE TO WOO US DEPENDING ON THE WEIGHT OF OUR SPITE ON THE SCALES OF YOUR LOVE. TELL US OUR SIN IF YOU REALLY MEAN TO DRIVE US AWAY IN CONFUSION.

HOUSE RULE 3:

IF WE ARE AFRAID THAT WE WILL SOON FALL FOR HIM, WE HIDE OURSELVES IN THE COMPANY OF OTHER QUEENS TO BARRICADE OUR PRIDE FROM THE WAVES OF HIS ADVANCES.

****

STRATEGY 3:

NEVER MAKE ADVANCES AT US WHEN WE ARE NOT ALONE. TALK GENERALLY AND IMPRESSIVELY. EVEN IF WE WANT YOU WHEN YOU MAKE SUCH PUBLIC ADVANCES, OUR OUTWARD ACTIONS WOULD SUGGEST WE HAVE A BETTER MAN MUCH FOR THE APPROVAL OF OUR EQUALLY PRETENTIOUS PEERS.

HOUSE RULE 4:

IF THE MAN WE ADORE DOES NOT LOOK US IN THE EYES OR ANYWHERE NEAR US, WE DO NOT GREET HIM EVEN IF WE ARE DYING TO DO SO.

****

STRATEGY 4:

WE EXCEL IN FAÇADES. IF YOU WANT US, LOOK US IN THE EYES. IF WE WANT YOU, YOUR LOOK WILL MAKE US MELT AT THE KNEES. WE FEAR THE EYES AS MUCH AS WE FEAR THE SOUND OF A MANLY VOICE IN OUR EARS. WE WOULD SURELY DO SOMETHING RESEMBLING SALUTATION UNLESS WE DO NOT WANT YOU OR WE WANT TO GET BACK AT YOU FOR BEING A SNOB BEFORE THEN.

HOUSE RULE 5:

WE PRETEND TO RESENT HIS PERSON AS A MATHEMATICAL REWARD IF HE IGNORES US.

****

STRATEGY 5:

WHEN WE IGNORE YOU, IT MAY BE BECAUSE YOU'VE DONE SO IN THE PAST. DO NOT DESPAIR. CONTINUE TO BE NICE BUT, FOR YOUR HONOUR, DO NOT WOO US IN DOING SO. HOWEVER, IF WE IGNORE YOU THE SECOND TIME, IT IS TIME FOR YOU TO DO LIKEWISE WHILE BEING NICE TO OTHER GIRLS AROUND US. IF YOU DO THIS AND WE ACTUALLY WANT YOU, WE WOULD GO THE FULL CIRCLE OR MATING DANCE OF SNOBBERY-RESENTMENT-DREAD-CURIOSITY FOR YOUR AMUSEMENT. WHEN WE GET TO CURIOSITY, WOO US AGAIN. UNFORTUNATELY, THE CIRCLE MAY TAKE YEARS DEPENDING ON THE NUMBER OF OUR ENCOUNTERS WITH YOU.

HOUSE RULE 6:

WE LOVE THE FAME, NOT THE MAN. BUT WE MAY END UP LOVING HIM AFTER ALL.

****

STRATEGY 6:

MAKE HAY WHILE THE SUN SHINES. CAPTURE OUR LOVE WHEN YOU HAVE NOT CREATED A WEB WITH MONEY OR ELSE YOU MAY DIG DEEPER FOR OUR LOVE. WHEN THE COMFORT OF YOUR FAME LURES US, GIVE US REASONS TO STAY IF AND WHEN THE FAME WILL FADE.

HOUSE RULE 7:

IF THE MAN WE ADORE PASSES BY US WHEN WE ARE WITH OUR FRIENDS, WE LAUGH MOCKINGLY AND LOUDLY AT NOTHING OR AS IF THERE IS SOMETHING ABOUT HIM WE ARE PRIVY TO, WHEN THERE IS NOTHING REALLY. THIS IS MEANT TO ATTRACT HIS ATTENTION TO US. AGAIN AND AGAIN, MOCKING LAUGHTER IS A WINNER ANY DAY. WE HIDE IN IT TO DISARM ANY MAN OR ANYTHING WE DO NOT UNDERSTAND. IT DOES NOT MATTER IF WE DO NOT HAVE ANY DESERVING REASON TO LAUGH.

SHOULD HE FAIL TO BE DRAWN BY OUR CALCULATED NOISE, WE FEEL A SENSE OF LOSS OR DESPAIR, BUT WE STIFLE IT.

****

STRATEGY 7:

IF YOU DISCOVER WE DO THIS EACH TIME YOU ARE AROUND, TRY STRATEGY 4. IF WE DO NOT RESPOND, RESORT TO STRATEGY 5 AND INCREASE YOUR CONTACTS WITH US TO QUICKEN THE SNOBBERY-RESENTMENT-DREAD-CURIOSITY CIRCLE OR MATING DANCE. WHEN WE GET TO CURIOSITY, STRIKE SOFTLY LIKE A GENTLEMAN, NOT A RAVENOUS WOLF.

HOUSE RULE 8:

WHEN IN A GATHERING, WE STOP TALKING TO OUR FRIENDS AND LISTEN WITH OUR EARS, NOT OUR EYES, WHEN THE MAN WE ADORE STARTS TALKING TO HIS FRIENDS ON THE OTHER TABLE.

****

STRATEGY 8:

WHEN YOU NOTICE THIS, SUPPRESS THE TEMPTATION TO RAISE THE DECIBELS OF YOUR VOICE FOR OUR BENEFIT. YOU WILL APPEAR OBNOXIOUS. JUST GO AHEAD, PRETENDING NOT TO NOTICE US. APPROACH US AT THE RIGHT TIME.

HOUSE RULE 9:

WE BRUSH PAST HIS SHOULDER, STEP ON HIS TOES OR BLOCK THE DOORWAY IF WE SENSE HE IS ABOUT TO USE THE DOOR. THEN WE APOLOGIZE WITH THE SWEETEST OF VOICE TO HAVE AN AVENUE TO TALK TO THE MAN WE ARE DYING TO HAVE THIS MINUTE.

****

STRATEGY 9:

UNLESS YOU ARE OCCUPIED WITH VOWS OF CELIBACY OR IN LOVE WITH SOMEONE ELSE, YOU NEED NO SOOTHSAYER TO RESPOND TO US. FURTHERMORE, WE WILL BE AT YOUR MERCY IF YOU RESPOND IN A SOFT, UNHURRIED MANNER UNLIKE WITH THE EARNESTNESS OF A WOLF. WHEN WE NEED YOU TO BE THAT EARNEST, YOU WILL KNOW .... BUT WATCH YOUR BACK TOO.

HOUSE RULE 10:

WE MOVE AWAY WITH OUR EYES OR OUR FEET IF A MAN BEGINS TO BLOW HIS TRUMPET AT THE WRONG TIME.

****

STRATEGY 10:

A MAN WHO BLOWS HIS TRUMPET ALWAYS IS EXHIBITING SIGNS OF INFERIORITY COMPLEX AND EFFEMINACY. WE ADORE MANLINESS IN ALL ITS RAMIFICATIONS. A TRUE WARRIOR SELDOM SPEAKS OF HOW MANY PEOPLE HE HAD KILLED IN BATTLE. IF HE DOES, IT WILL BE DURING NECESSARY MOMENTS. IN FACT, WE, THE WOMENFOLK, SPREAD THE NEWS. YOUR SILENT AIR OF IMPORTANCE IS ENOUGH FOR US TO KNOW HOW DEEPLY NOBLE YOU ARE.

HOUSE RULE 11:

WE WRIGGLE OUR HIPS AS WE WALK IF WE SENSE HE IS LOOKING AT OUR BEHIND.

****

STRATEGY 11:

THIS MAY BE A PLOY TO (1) CAPTURE AND/OR DESTROY YOU (2) MAKE YOU QUENCH A CRAVING.... AND/OR (3) MAKE YOU LOVE US AS WE DO YOU. APPLY STRATEGY 9 OR MOVE TO 7 DEPENDING ON OUR NEXT MOVE AFTER YOUR 9. OF COURSE, DO THIS ONLY IF YOU ARE GAME.

HOUSE RULE 12:

WE LOOK LONGINGLY AT HIM TO DRAW HIS EYES TO OUR BODY IF WE WANT HIM NOW.

****

STRATEGY 12:

THIS IS OUR MOST COMMON PLOY.   SEE STRATEGY 11.

HOUSE RULE 13:

WE BEGIN TO SING LOVINGLY AS HE PASSES BY
OR STAND IN HIS LINE OF VISION SO THAT HE WOULD
INEVITABLY LOOK AT US – IF HE IS WORTH IT.

****

STRATEGY 13:
SEE STRATEGY 11.

HOUSE RULE 14:

EVEN IF WE MEAN TO, WE NEVER SAY "YES" TO HIM THE VERY FIRST TIME HE REQUESTS TO BE OUR INTIMATE FRIEND. THIS WOULD GIVE US TIME TO UNDERSTUDY HIM. NEVERTHELESS, WE DO NOT GIVE HIM THE COLD SHOULDER RECEPTION.

****

STRATEGY 14:

IF WE DO THIS, DO NOT DESPAIR. MAKE A MANLY SHOW OF PERSISTENCE. YOUR AMOUNT OF PERSISTENCE AND COMMITMENT WOULD ATTRACT AN EQUAL AMOUNT OF CONSIDERATION FROM US. WE ARE ONLY TESTING THE RELIABILITY OF THE ROCK OF YOUR LOVE ON THE TURBULENT WATERS OF LIFE. ELSE, WE HAVE PUT YOU IN SUSPENSE, FRUSTRATING YOUR DESIRE, LEAVING NO ROOM FOR YOU TO GO FOR ANOTHER GIRL AND MAKING YOU RUN AMOK TO DO OUR BIDDING. USE THE MIRROR EFFECT TO REVERSE THE SUSPENSE. APPLY STRATEGY 11.

HOUSE RULE 15:

IF WE SENSE URGENCY IN OUR MAN TO MAKE LOVE TO US AFTER WE JUST BEGIN DATING EACH OTHER, HE IS EITHER VERY MUCH IN LOVE WITH US AND WANTS TO EXPRESS IT THAT WAY OR HE IS AFTER OUR BODY OR HAVE BOTH FEELINGS. WE USUALLY BUY TIME TO DECIDE WHICH INTENTION HE HAS OR WE GIVE IN TO PRESSURE IF THE FEROCIOUSNESS OF HIS ADVANCE SWALLOWS OUR RESISTANCE.

****

STRATEGY 15:

IF WE GIVE IN TO YOU THE VERY FIRST DAY OR A FEW DAYS AFTER WE BEGIN TO DATE, WE ARE EITHER IN THE EXTREME OF NOT LOVING YOU AT ALL OR IN THE OTHER EXTREME OF LOVING YOU SO VERY MUCH. EXPECT REACTIONS FROM US BASED ON EITHER OF THESE TWO EXTREMES AND ALSO ON YOUR OWN INTENTIONS.

HOUSE RULE 16:

WE OPEN OUR LEGS AND GUIDE HIS EYES TO OUR CENTRE IF WE CAN'T WAIT ANYMORE.

****

STRATEGY 16:
SEE STRATEGY 11.

HOUSE RULE 17:

WE MOVE TO THE MAN THAT CONTROLS BUT CARES FOR US AND AWAY FROM THE MAN THAT SHOWS SIGNS OF WEAKNESS AND NON-COMMITMENT.

****

STRATEGY 17:

WE ARE SAFER THAT WAY. THIS IS ALSO A STRONG SURVIVAL MOVE TO PROTECT OUR GENES FROM WEAK INTRUSION AND TO REPRODUCE THEM IF NEED BE.

HOUSE RULE 18:

WE CROSS OUR LEGS ALWAYS WHEN WE SIT DOWN. BUT WE MAY DANCE IN OUR CHAIR WHEN THE ADORABLE MAN IS AROUND.

****

STRATEGY 18:

IF WE BEHAVE IN THIS MANNER, THEN WE WOULD DEFINITELY SAY "YES" IF YOU ASK US OUT AND WE WOULD BE READY FOR YOUR LOVE IF NEED BE.

HOUSE RULE 19:

WE SPLASH MUD ON THE MAN THAT IGNORES US AND WE PRETEND NOT TO NOTICE.

****

STRATEGY 19:

IF YOU WANT US, APPLY STRATEGY 5. IF NOT, JUST KNOW THAT WE COURT ATTENTION BY NATURE. ASIDE FROM THE POSSIBILITY THAT WE MAY BE INTENT ON INVERTED LOVE, WE ARE GENERALLY UNSETTLED IF WE ARE IGNORED. THE EMOTIONAL CYCLE DEFINITELY BEGINS. IT DOES NOT MATTER WHETHER WE WANT YOU OR NOT.

HOUSE RULE 20:

WE PRETEND TO BE WEAK OR IN PAINS SO THAT ANY MAN AROUND WHO WE LIKE OR WHO LIKES US WOULD LIFT THE BURDEN WE ARE SUPPOSED TO HANDLE.

****

STRATEGY 20:

BECAUSE WE ARE WEAKER IN TERMS OF PHYSICAL STRENGTH, WE SOMETIMES FORCE YOUR ATTENTION TO US BY FEIGNING A BOGUS DEGREE OF WEAKNESS EITHER TO GET YOU TO DO SOMETHING FOR US OR TO GET YOU INTERESTED IN US BY SUBTERFUGE. BALANCE THIS BY INSISTING ON US GETTING OUT OUR ASSETS.

HOUSE RULE 21:

WE MAY HAVE MORE FURY THAN HELL WHEN A MAN SCORNS US.

****

STRATEGY 21:

EVEN IF YOU HATE US, DO NOT DO MORE THAN SNOBBERY. WE MAY NEVER STOP UNTIL WE HIT BACK IF YOUR TONGUE LASHES OUT AT US. WE MAY BE SUBDUED IF AND ONLY IF WE ARE HELPLESSLY IN LOVE WITH YOU OR TOTALLY LOST IN YOUR STRENGTH OF PRESENCE.

HOUSE RULE 22:

WE GYRATE TOWARDS ANY RELIABLE MAN AROUND WHENEVER WE SENSE A PHYSICAL DANGER.

****

STRATEGY 22:

IF A BOMB DROPS NEARBY, WE WOULD BE ALL OVER YOU BEFORE YOU KNOW WHAT HITS YOU. THIS IS JUST A NATURAL REACTION. IT MAY OR MAY NOT INDICATE LOVE FOR YOU.

HOUSE RULE 23:

WHEN WE SENSE THAT A MAN IS A CELIBATE, WE THRONG TO HIM.

* * * * * * * * *

STRATEGY 23:

WE ADORE YOU IF YOU DO NOT CARE ABOUT OUR BODY. WE SUSPECT YOU KNOW THE GREATEST SECRET (SEE STRATEGY 37) AND WE THRONG TO YOU BECAUSE WE VALUE YOU IF YOU PRICE YOURSELF VERY HIGH. MOREOVER, WE TRUST YOU IF YOU REGARD SEX AS NOT THE PRIMARY BASIS FOR A RELATIONSHIP. HOWEVER, WATCH OUT, WE MAY BE DILUTERS.

HOUSE RULE 24:

COME WHAT MAY, WE CALL THE FINAL SHOT AND WIN THE SILENT SIDE OF THE GAME, HOWEVER UNNOTICEABLE IT APPEARS

****

STRATEGY 24:

YOU REGALE YOURSELF WITH THE OBVIOUS. YES, YOU EASILY FORGET THAT THOUGH ROME OBVIOUSLY CONQUERED ANCIENT GREECE, THE LATTER'S CULTURE CONQUERED ROME IN THE LONG RUN, NOW, WHO WON? BE CAREFUL! THE CLEOPATRA IN US CAN SUBDUE ANY JULIUS CAESAR.... *PUT YOUR EYES TO THE GROUND AND PICK THE TRACES OF YOUR HURRY IN THE EUPHORIA OF OBVIOUS VICTORY.*

HOUSE RULE 25:

WE MAINTAIN AN EFFECTIVE GOSSIP CIRCLE WHEREVER WE CONGREGATE. THIS HELPS US KNOW THE MASCULINE SCAPEGOAT IN VOGUE.

****

STRATEGY 25:

IF YOU SUSPECT YOU ARE THE MARK, BEGIN IMMEDIATELY TO PRICE YOURSELF MUCH HIGHER THAN BEFORE. DO NOT GIVE US REASONS TO INTENSIFY OUR IDLE CHATTER. THE POPULARITY WE HAVE CREATED FOR YOU CAN BE PUT TO GOOD USE IN CONFUSING AND DISARMING US WHEN ALL CURIOUS EYES ARE STILL ON YOU.

HOUSE RULE 26:

COMFORT IS GOOD. THEREFORE, WE GO AFTER COMFORT, NOT THE MAN. WELL, WE MAY END UP LOVING HIM AFTER ALL.

****

STRATEGY 26:

MONEY CAN BUY A COMFORTABLE

ENVIRONMENT. NOW, IF YOUR MIND IS ALSO AT PEACE WITH THIS ENVIRONMENT, WE WOULD DO ANYTHING TO HANG ON TO YOU. IT IS THE GOOD WE SEE AROUND AND IN YOU THAT WE WILL MISS IF AND WHEN WE HAVE A QUARREL WITH YOU. THE MEMORIES WOULD HAUNT US SO MUCH THAT YOU MAY SEE US AT YOUR DOOR AGAIN.

HOUSE RULE 27:

WE BEHAVE AS IF WE EXPECT A MAN TO REACT TO A PRESENT CONVERSATION. IF HE DOES, WE IGNORE HIM WITH AN EMBARRASSING PAUSE. IF HE DOES NOT, WE SPREAD THE WORD THAT HE IS RIGID. EITHER WAY, THE POINT IS TO NAIL HIM.

****

STRATEGY 27:

THIS MAY BE A SIGN OF RESENTMENT IN THE MATING DANCE WE PUT UP FOR YOU. IT CAN ALSO BE A GENUINE EFFORT TO TEAR YOU TO SHREDS. DETERMINE WHICH ONE IT IS BY INCREASING YOUR CONTACTS WITH US WITHOUT APPEARING TO DO SO— IF YOU CARE.... SEE STRATEGY 5.

HOUSE RULE 28:

LIKE THE EVER CLIMBING IVY, WE HAVE SPREAD OUR OLD STRATAGEM AROUND OUR NEW WEAPON: THE MOBILE PHONE. WE MAY NOT CALL YOU AS OFTEN AS YOU DO US.

****

STRATEGY 28:

WE LOVE THE MOBILE PHONE BECAUSE WE CRAVE FOR YOUR VOICE. HOWEVER, WE WILL NOT CALL YOU THE WAY YOU MAY WANT US TO: WE WANT TO REMAIN THE HUNTED, FOR WE ENJOY BEING CHASED AND WE ENJOY BEING SPENT FOR. THE AMOUNT OF CALLS YOU MAKE AFFECTS US PSYCHOLOGICALLY. YOUR VOICE KEEPS RINGING.... LOOK FOR A WAY OF MAKING MORE CALLS WHILE SPENDING LESS. IF YOU SUDDENLY STOP CALLING AFTER DOING SO FOR A LONG TIME AND IF THERE ARE NO OTHER VOICES LIKE YOURS, WE WOULD COME AFTER YOU BECAUSE YOUR VOICE HAS BECOME ADDICTIVE.

HOUSE RULE 29:

WE WOULD NEVER DISCLOSE ANY OF OUR SECRET PRINCIPLES TO THOSE WE INTEND TO USE THEM ON. WE MODIFY OUR PRINCIPLES FOR USE ON MEN WHO ALREADY ARE AWARE OF THE SIMPLE ONES. WE SUCCUMB TO MEN WHO REMAIN UNBOWED.

****

STRATEGY 29:

WHEN YOU UNDERSTAND OUR POWERS AND DISPLAY YOUR KNOWLEDGE OF THEM, YOU MAY ATTRACT OUR ATTENTION POSITIVELY OR NEGATIVELY—DEPENDING ON WHY YOU CARRY OUT SUCH A DISPLAY OF WEAPONS AND HOW SELF-EFFACING YOU ARE IN SUCH ACTIONS. IF YOU ARE NAÏVE, STUDY OUR ACTIONS AND BOOKS LIKE THIS ONE IN YOUR HANDS AND ARM YOURSELF WITH PRACTICAL KNOWLEDGE. DO NOT UNDERESTIMATE US.

HOUSE RULE 30:

WE MOVE AWAY FROM WEAK AND EFFUSIVELY POLITE MEN TO STRONG, CONFIDENT AND RELIABLE MEN, I.E. MEN WHO SHOW EVIDENCE OF BEING AMONG THE FITTEST OF MEN WITHOUT HOOTING THEIR TRUMPETS.

****

STRATEGY 30:

SORRY, THIS IS A STRONG SURVIVAL MOVE TO PROTECT AND REPRODUCE OUR GENES IF NEED BE. IT ALSO IS A MOVE TO ACQUIRE SECURITY AND STABILITY. STRIVE TO BE AMONG THE BEST OF MEN. YOUR INVOLVEMENT IN SPORTS MAY OR MAY NOT ATTRACT US, DEPENDING ON THE DIGNITY OF YOUR MIND AND THE GRACE OF YOUR BODY. WE STRIVE FOR INTELLIGENCE, POPULARITY, PROGRESS, NEAT APPEARANCE, VISION, CALMNESS AND FIRMNESS IN MAN.

HOUSE RULE 31:

SAD MEN MAY NOT ATTRACT OUR REAL LOVE. THEY MAY ONLY ATTRACT OUR SYMPATHY, WHICH MAY BE MISTAKEN FOR LOVE. SECONDLY, UNNECESSARILY TACITURN MEN ATTRACT OUR GENUINE DREAD.

****

STRATEGY 31:

BE HUMOROUS WITHOUT BEING A COURT JESTER. WE LOVE WHAT MAKES US HAPPY. YOUR COURAGE TO BE HAPPY WHATEVER THE SITUATION SWEEPS US OFF OUR FEET. SECONDLY, OUR EARS CRAVE FOR YOUR TONGUE AS YOUR EYES CRAVE FOR OUR BODY. YOU CAN UNDO US WITH YOUR TONGUE AND EYES. WE CAN UNDO YOU WITH OUR BODY. YOU CAN SHUT YOUR EYES. WE CANNOT SHUT OUR EARS.

HOUSE RULE 32:

WE DO NOT LOVE MEN WHO DO NOT LOVE WHAT WE LOVE.

****

STRATEGY 32:

COMMONALITY OF INTEREST, ESPECIALLY IN AREAS OF RELIGION, PHILOSOPHY, POLITICS, CAREER AND POTENTIALITIES, IS THE KEY TO A LASTING RELATIONSHIP. LOVE WHAT WE LOVE AND WE WOULD FALL FOR YOU.

HOUSE RULE 33:

WE LOVE MEN WHO FILL GAPS IN OUR TEMPERAMENTS.

****

STRATEGY 33:

TRY TO FIND OUT WHAT TEMPERAMENT WE POSSESS. ARE WE *PREDOMINANTLY* SANGUINE, CHOLERIC, MELANCHOLIC OR PHLEGMATIC? GIVE US REASONS TO BELIEVE YOU ARE HERE TO GRAPPLE WITH OUR INSECURITIES WHEN YOU FIND OUT WHAT TEMPERAMENTAL BLEND WE POSSESS.

HOUSE RULE 34:

WE CAN GET INTENSELY SATISFIED AND MAKE DO WITH ONLY HEAVY PETTING, WITHOUT THE MAIN-COURSE: SEX.

****

STRATEGY 34:

BECAUSE WE ARE SATISFIED WITH THE PENUMBRA TO SEX, YOU MAY FEEL FRUSTRATED. THIS IS GENERALLY OUR NATURE. TAKE US THERE GENTLY; DO NOT SHOW SIGNS OF URGENCY. IF YOU DO, WE'LL RUN.

HOUSE RULE 35:

WE ARE THE HANDMAIDS OF MOODS. WE MAY NOT RESPOND TO THE ADVANCES OR STRATEGIES OF MEN AT PARTICULAR MOMENTS IN SPACE AND TIME.

****

STRATEGY 35:

NOTICE HOW, DURING PLAYTIME, A CHILD BEGINS TO CRY FOR FOOD OR OUT OF BOREDOM, MINUTES AFTER ENJOYING THE SAME THING YOU ARE STILL DOING TO KEEP HER HAPPY. WATCH OUR MOODS AND STRIKE AT THE RIGHT TIME OR ELSE WE MAY EXPLODE IF YOU DO NOT HANDLE US WITH CARE.

HOUSE RULE 36:

ON FIRST CONTACT OR WHEN WE WORK FOR HIM, WE ARE SORRY FOR THE MAN WHO POURS OUT HIS AFFECTION ON US WITHOUT A SHOW OF RESTRAINT.

****

STRATEGY 36:

WE ARE LIKE YOUR SHADOW AND YOUR SWORD. IF YOU CAPTURE OUR AFFECTIONS WITHOUT BETRAYING YOUR EMOTIONS, YOU HAVE TAKEN YOUR SWORD BY THE HANDLE AND CAN PUT US TO EFFECTIVE USE. IF YOU BETRAY YOUR EMOTIONS AND WE ARE NOT CAPTURED IN THAT BID, YOU ARE AT OUR MERCY AND ARE HANDLING THE BLADE.... WHEN YOU MOVE, YOUR SHADOW FOLLOWS ALONG. WHEN YOU GO AFTER YOUR SHADOW, IT RUNS INFINITELY.

HOUSE RULE 37:

WE ARE PRIVY TO A GREAT SECRET: WE ENJOY SEX MORE DEEPLY THAN MEN AND THAN THEY THINK.

****

STRATEGY 37:

ASIDE FROM THE FACT THAT SOCIETY CONDITIONS US TO CONCEAL THIS FACT, YOU ARE LESS ABLE TO ENDURE THE CRAVING. THUS, WE WOULD NOTE YOU AS THE MAN TO GO FOR IF YOU VALUE YOUR BODY AS MUCH AS WE DO OURS.

HOUSE RULE 38:

A POOR MAN CAN WIN OUR LOVE IF HE IS ROMANTIC.

****

STRATEGY 38:

WE VALUE ROMANCE MUCH MORE THAN WE DO MONEY. IF WHAT IS IN YOU IS GREATER THAN MONEY, YOU WILL HAVE US GUNNING FOR YOU.

HOUSE RULE 39:

WE MOVE AWAY FROM A MAN WHO APPEARS LIKE A SHIP CAST ADRIFT AND THRONG TO THE MAN FOR WHOM THE WORLD MAKES WAY BECAUSE HE KNOWS WHERE HE IS GOING.

****

STRATEGY 39:

MOST WOMEN, IF NOT ALL, WANT A SECURE AND SETTLED LIFE. DISCOVER YOURSELF, THEN DRAW UP A LIFETIME GOAL IN LINE WITH YOUR DISCOVERY, AND FOLLOW IT. YOU WILL BE THE DREAM OF EVERY WOMAN WITHOUT EVEN TRYING.

HOUSE RULE 40:

SADLY, WE ARE UNEXCITED AROUND A MAN WHOSE INTELLIGENCE QUOTIENT IS LOWER THAN OURS.

****

STRATEGY 40:

WE WILL DREAM ABOUT YOU EXCITEDLY IF YOU ARE A WALKING ENCYCLOPAEDIA WITHOUT APPEARING OBNOXIOUS.

HOUSE RULE 41:

OF COURSE, WE MOVE AWAY FROM MEN WHO APPEAR DIRTY AT FIRST SIGHT.

****

STRATEGY 41:

PRIMA FACIE, YOUR APPEARANCE IS AS IMPORTANT TO US AS OURS IS TO YOU. DRESS NEATLY AND RESPONSIBLY.

HOUSE RULE 42:

THOUGH WE ARE INTERESTED IN MEN, WE DO NOT INITIATE THE OBVIOUS ASPECT OF THIS INTEREST. MEN MUST DO THE CHASING.

****

STRATEGY 42:

DO NOT KILL YOURSELF BEGGING US TO BE YOUR SPOUSE. IF WE DO NOT SHOW INTEREST, EXAMINE US TO KNOW WHAT WE ARE UP TO. ARE WE UNDERSTUDYING YOU OR ARE WE CREATING A CONDITION IN WHICH YOU MAY BECOME OUR SLAVE? PRESSURE US WITH YOUR TENDER VOICE AS YOU TALK ABOUT OTHER ISSUES UNTIL YOU SOFTEN US UP.

HOUSE RULE 43:

IN LESS PERMISSIVE CULTURES, WE NEVER VOICE OUT OUR LOVE AND/ OR LONGING FOR A MAN, OUR BODY LANGUAGE SUGGESTS OUR INTERESTS.

****

STRATEGY 43:

LEARN TO DECIPHER OUR BODY LANGUAGE. WE SPEAK LESS AT THE BEGINNING OF A RELATIONSHIP. THEREFORE, OBSERVE OUR EYES, POSTURE, COMPOSURE AND OTHER NON-VERBAL COMMUNICATION. CONSIDER US AND BE WISE. SEE STRATEGY 11.

HOUSE RULE 44:

WE ARE PRONE TO BELIEVE THAT MEN ARE VERY RESPONSIVE TO GUT-LEVEL URGES; THEIR ID DOES NOT COME THROUGH SOCIAL FINESSE. NO MATTER THEIR STATUS IN SOCIETY, THEY ARE VERY SIMILAR IN THEIR LOW WILL-POWER IN THE AREA OF SEXUAL SELF-CONTROL.

****

STRATEGY 44:

THIS BELIEF OF OURS COMES FROM OUR CONSTANT EXPERIENCE WITH MEN. TRY TO PROVE THAT YOU ARE WITHIN THE SMALL CIRCLE OF MEN WHO CANNOT BE MANIPULATED BECAUSE OF THE DESIRE FOR ORGASM AND OTHER PLEASURES OF SEX. YOU'LL GAIN OUR RESPECT FOR THIS. THE MORE YOU SHOW YOU HAVE NO TIME FOR OUR BODY, THE STRONGER WILL BE OUR INTEREST IN YOU. SOME OF US MAY NOT LIKE THIS STANCE. BUT, DOES IT MATTER? OUR LIKING OR DISLIKING YOU DOES LITTLE TO CONTRIBUTE TO YOUR PROGRESS—UNLESS IF YOU LOVE US. MOREOVER, YOUR LIFE WILL BE MORE PRODUCTIVE AND READY FOR THE BEST OF US. IN CHOOSING US, YOU WILL GO FOR ASSETS AND NOT LIABILITIES.

HOUSE RULE 45:

WE EITHER DO NOT SEND TEXT MESSAGES OR SEND ANY THAT BETRAYS ANY INTIMATE FEELING TO A MAN EVEN WHEN WE ARE INTERESTED IN HIM. WE FOIL ANY POSSIBLE EVIDENCE OF OUR INTEREST IN HIM. IF AND WHEN WE REPLY, WE ARE AMBIGUOUS.

****

STRATEGY 45:

IF YOU WANT US, YOUR VOICE IS IMPORTANT. BUT IF WE CONTINUE TO BE ALOOF. IT IS TIME TO PLACE A CHECKMATE. SEND US A TEXT MESSAGE THAT WILL NEED A RESPONDER. IF WE FALL INTO THAT TRAP AND RESPOND TO IT. STOP THERE. THE FIRST AND/OR LAST PERSON TO SEND A TEXT MESSAGE IS THE UNDERDOG WHOSE ACTION HAS BEEN IGNORED— THOUGH WE MAY SEND THE LAST TEXT IF IT IS A STINKER DURING A QUARREL.

HOUSE RULE 46:

WE ARE AWARE THAT MEN LOVE TO THINK THEY ARE POWERFUL. THEREFORE, WE MAKE SURE WE ALLOW THEM TO FEEL SECURE AND COMFORTABLE WITH US, EVEN IF THEY BEHAVE LIKE CHILDREN WHO ARE REINFORCED BY PELLETS FROM US AND FRUSTRATED IF WE DO NOT GIVE THEM ANY.

****

STRATEGY 46:

WE WOULD BE WARY OF YOU IF YOU DO NOT RESPOND TO OUR SENSUAL PELLETS. IT SHOWS YOU ARE A FOCUSED MAN.   CAREFULLY WATCH OUR WORDS TO NOTE IF WE REALLY THINK YOU ARE POWERFUL. UNGUARDED SNATCHES OF JEST FROM US WOULD REVEAL THIS, ESPECIALLY WHEN WE FEEL FREE IN YOUR PRESENCE. BEHAVE LIKE A FOOL TO MAKE US UNGUARDED.

HOUSE RULE 47:

ON CONTACT WITH MEN, WE ARE INCLINED TO DISCOVER THEIR WEAKNESSES OR SOFT SPOTS. IT IS BY LOWERING OUR ANCHORS ONTO THESE SPOTS THAT WE MOOR THE MAN. OUR ANCHORS ARE, AMONG OTHERS, THE KITCHEN, UPPER AND LOWER SEX ORGANS, CAT WALKS, EYES, EYE LASHES AND TONE OF VOICE.

****

STRATEGY 47:

DISCOVER YOURSELF BEFORE SOMEONE ELSE DOES. KNOW AND WORK ON YOUR WEAKNESSES. BE SWIFT AND CREATIVE IN FOILING OUR MOVES TO CONQUER YOU. A MESS OF POTTAGE IS WORTH MORE THAN A CONQUERED MAN.

HOUSE RULE 48:

BLACKMAIL IS A WONDERFUL VICE. WE USE THIS TO GET THE MAN TO HIS KNEES. FOR EXAMPLE, MAIDS CAN THREATEN TO REVEAL THE SEXUAL ABNORMALITIES OF A MAN TO HIS WIFE.

****

STRATEGY 48:

BE CAREFUL HOW YOU INTERACT WITH US. WE NEVER FORGET SPOKEN WORDS. WE SEE APOLOGIES AS WINDOW DRESSING. IF WE TRY TO BLACKMAIL YOU, RESIST IT TO THE BAREST MINIMUM. AFTER ALL, IT TAKES TWO TO TANGO.

HOUSE RULE 49:

WE CALL ALL MEN WHO *EFFUSIVELY* DO THINGS FOR US FOOLS.

****

STRATEGY 49:

BE FIRM AND NICE YET IMPORTANT. DO NOT MEET *SOME* OF OUR NEEDS AS AT THE TIME WE WANT THEM MET AND DO NOT MEET THEM THE WAY WE WANT THEM MET. SURPRISE US WITH OCCASIONAL EFFUSIVE CARE. BE THE FINAL DETERMINANT OF THE CONTENT AND FORM OF YOUR CARE.

HOUSE RULE 50:

LIKE MEN, WE TOO TELL HALF-TRUTHS OR LIE WHEN WE FEEL THAT TELLING THE TRUTH WOULD PUT US IN A POSITION OF NOT BEING APPRECIATED OR ACCEPTED. WE ARE MERCURIAL TOO. IF WE MEAN TO SAY "YES", WE SAY, "MAY BE". IF WE ARE CONFUSED, WE SAY "I DON'T KNOW". NEVERTHELESS, OUR "NO" IS USUALLY "NO".

****

STRATEGY 50:

EXAMINE EVERYTHING WE SAY. COMPARE THIS WITH THINGS WE SAID BEFORE, THINGS OTHER PEOPLE TELL YOU AND THINGS YOU GLEANED FROM PSYCHOLOGICAL AND RELIGIOUS TEXTS. DO NOT TOLERATE LIES. GENTLY MAKE US RECOGNIZE OUR ERRORS. IF WE PERSIST IN THEM, AND YOU ARE HONEST YOURSELF, THEN YOU CAN THROW THE STONE, THAT IS, PUNISH US. WE MAY BE BETTER AFTER THAT.

HOUSE RULE 51:

RECEIVING ATTENTION AND APPRECIATION IS MORE CENTRAL TO OUR SURVIVAL AND SUCCESS. WE CAN DO ANYTHING TO GET THEM FROM MEN.

****

STRATEGY 51:

BE GENEROUS WITH WORDS OF APPRECIATION. BE TACTICAL AND SELECTIVE WITH GIVING ATTENTION. YOU CAN WITHDRAW APPRECIATION AND ATTENTION AT WILL JUST TO BE IN CONTROL. WE LOVE CONTROL. THUS, WE WOULD BE SUBMISSIVE TO YOU.

HOUSE RULE 52:

ALMOST ALL OF US WERE ONCE CONSCIOUS OR UNCONSCIOUS PROTÉGÉS OF OUR MOTHERS IN THE ART OF HOUSE RULES, SUBTLE OR OTHERWISE.

****

STRATEGY 52:

LEARN OUR HOUSE RULES AND USE THEM AGAINST US IN A "MIRROR-EFFECT" MANNER. ASIDE FROM THIS BOOK, THERE ARE MANY OTHER BOOKS DETAILING OUR CASUISTRY WITHOUT NAMING THEM DIRECTLY. READ THEM. SEE SUGGESTIONS FOR FURTHER READINGS.

HOUSE RULE 53:

THOUGH WE ENJOY SEX MORE DEEPLY THAN DO MEN, WE DO NOT SEE IT AS IMPORTANT AS TO MAKE MEN BREAK THEIR NECKS FOR IT. AFTER ALL, IT LASTS FOR NOT MORE THAN FIVE MINUTES. NEVERTHELESS, WE PRETEND IT IS SO PRECIOUS IN ORDER THAT MEN WILL CONTINUE ANGLING FOR IT AT VERY GREAT COSTS.

****

STRATEGY 53:

IF YOU UNDERSTAND THIS FACT, YOU WILL BE ON THE TOP OF THE WORLD. FOR WHAT DOES IT PROFIT YOU TO PAY AN AWESOME PRICE FOR A THING AS FLEETING AS SEX? ARE YOU NOT A FOOL OF THE HIGHEST ORDER?

HOUSE RULE 54:

WE TAKE PRIDE IN THE FACT THAT, THOUGH WE ARE PHYSICALLY WEAKER THAN MEN, WE ARE EMOTIONALLY MORE MATURE AND STRONGER THAN THEY ARE. IN THE CHRISTIAN TEXT, WE BROUGHT THE WISEST MAN, SOLOMON, AND THE STRONGEST MAN, SAMSON, TO THEIR KNEES. CLEOPATRA, BILHAH, DELILAH, SHUAH, TAMAR AND BATHSHEBA ARE OUR ROLE MODELS....

****

STRATEGY 54:

ARM YOURSELF AGAINST OUR UNMISTAKABLE POWERS. GO TO HISTORY AND LEARN. IN OUR PRESENCE, TAKE NOTHING FOR GRANTED.

HOUSE RULE 55:

WE MAY GIVE SEX TO MEN JUST TO CONTROL AND GET SOMETHING MUCH MORE IMPORTANT TO US FROM THEM. WE DO THIS AND ENSURE THAT THEY DO NOT TAKE AWAY THEIR MINDS FROM US. WE ARE WARY AND BEMUSED BY THE HIGH VALUE MEN HAVE PLACED ON SEX.

****

STRATEGY 55:

IF YOU DO NOT WANT TO BE A TOY IN OUR HANDS, BEGIN FROM THIS MOMENT TO SEE SEX AS NOT-WORTH-THE-PRIZE YOU HAD HITHERTO PLACED ON IT. IT IS ONLY WORTH THE WHILE AND ONE WAY OF EXPRESSION WHEN TWO PEOPLE ARE EQUALLY IN LOVE WITH EACH OTHER. WE WILL KEEP YOU AT ALL COST IF WE DISCOVER THAT YOU HAVE SELF-CONTROL.

HOUSE RULE 56:

WE ARE MASTERS AT THE ETERNAL PRACTICE OF CONSERVATION OF ENERGY. THEREFORE, WE TEND TO LIVE LONGER THAN MEN DO. DURING LOVE MAKING, WE MAKE MEN DO ALL THE WORK WHILE WE RECEIVE THE PLEASURE.

****

STRATEGY 56:

LEARN TO SLEEP WITHOUT US IN BED WITH YOU ALWAYS. IF YOU MARRY US, YOU MAY MAKE US HAVE A DIFFERENT ROOM IF YOU DO NOT TRUST YOUR WILL POWER. YOU NEED TO TRANSMUTE EXCESS LIBIDINAL ENERGY TO CREATIVE ENERGY FOR MORE IMPORTANT THINGS IN YOUR LIFE LIKE WRITING BOOKS AND INVENTING THINGS, WHICH WOULD OUTLAST YOU.

HOUSE RULE 57:

WE PERCEIVE THAT MEN ARE VERY FOOLISH WHEN LOVE OVERTAKES THEM. THEY TEND TO DO ANYTHING FOR US IN THIS CONDITION AND WE ARE QUITE "IMPRESSED" INDEED. THUS, WHEN WE MEET ONE THAT DOES NOT FIT THIS DESCRIPTION, WE CAN GO ANY LENGTH TO MAKE THE MAN COMPROMISE HIS ALOOFNESS....

****

STRATEGY 57:

MAN, REFUSE TO BE FOOLISH FOR ANYONE UNDER ANY EMOTIONAL SPELL, UNLESS YOU ARE INSANE. LEARN TO BE AN EMOTION MANAGER. WATCH OUT FOR THE VARIOUS ATTEMPTS WE EMPLOY TO INFLUENCE YOU: IF YOU ARE OUR HUSBAND, ESPECIALLY IN MODERN AFRICAN CULTURE, WE SERVE YOU FOOD LATE; WE REFUSE TO SERVE YOU THE FOOD OF YOUR CHOICE; WE BROOD OVER PETTY ISSUES IN THE HOUSE AND WE MAY DENY YOU SEX.

HOUSE RULE 58:

DURING LOVEMAKING, MEN TEND TO ALLOW THEIR LOGICAL THOUGHT PROCESSES FLY OUT OF THE WINDOW. AT SUCH MOMENTS, WE SEE WINDOWS OF OPPORTUNITIES OPEN UP FOR US. WE ENSURE THEY KEEP PROMISES THEY MAKE AT SUCH MOMENTS IF THEY ARE TO GET ANOTHER CHANCE.

****

STRATEGY 58:

SEE STRATEGIES 53, 55, 56.

HOUSE RULE 59:

JUST AS A FISH SENSES THE INTRODUCTION OF ANOTHER LIQUID INTO ITS LAKE, WE SENSE WHEN OUR MAN BECOMES INTERESTED IN ANOTHER WOMAN. AMONG OTHER SIMPLE THINGS, HIS ATTENTION WOULD NO LONGER BE CONCENTRATED ON US.

****

STRATEGY 59:

LIKE AN ECONOMIST, DECIDE YOUR OPPORTUNITY COST AND SCALE OF PREFERENCE.

HOUSE RULE 60:

WE TAKE THE GAME OF GETTING AND KEEPING A MAN AS REAL WAR. WE EMPLOY ALL THE SKILLS AND KNOWLEDGE IN OUR DISPOSAL TO DO THIS. WE GENERALLY DO NOT LIKE TO SHARE THE MAN WE LOVE. WE MAY SHARE THE MAN WE DO NOT LOVE.

****

STRATEGY 60:

WHEN WE FIGHT FOR YOU, REFUSE TO TAKE SIDES. FIND A WAY OF BECOMING VERY IMPORTANT WITHOUT APPEARING OBNOXIOUS DURING THIS FIGHT. FROM THE PERSPECTIVE OF THE BONE OF CONTENTION AND POSSIBLE CONSEQUENCES OF MAKING MISTAKES, DECIDE ON WHO TO ELIMINATE AND DO SO WITHOUT QUALMS.

HOUSE RULE 61:

WE MAKE MEN PAY FOR SEX IN MANY WAYS OTHER THAN WITH MONEY.

****

STRATEGY 61:

IF YOU UNDERSTAND THAT THE TWO PARTIES INVOLVED IN SEX SHARE IN ITS ENJOYMENT, YOU WILL WAKE UP FROM PAYING FOR IT ALONE.

HOUSE RULE 62:

WE LIKE TO HEAR SECRETS. MEN LIKE TO SHARE SECRETS. WE MAY USE THESE SECRETS TO OUR ADVANTAGE IN ORDER TO MAKE US SUPERIOR TO MEN.

****

STRATEGY 62:

LEARN THE ART OF CALCULATED SPEECH. SPEAK LESS THAN NECESSARY. DURING MOMENTS OF EUPHORIA, WE ARE ABLE TO SCAN AWAY EMOTIONS AND BRING OUT THE REAL MEANING OF WHAT YOU SAY, IT DOES NOT MATTER WHETHER YOU SAID IT WHILE LAUGHING OR CRYING. AGAIN AND AGAIN, WE WILL BRING ABOUT THE SAME SITUATION THAT INTRODUCES EUPHORIA IN ORDER TO DISARM YOU TO OUR ADVANTAGE.

HOUSE RULE 63:

WE PREFER TO BE IN THE COMPANY OF MEN BECAUSE THEY GIVE US ROOM TO SHINE LIKE THE SUN IN THEIR PRESENCE. WE FIGHT WITH ONE ANOTHER FOR ATTENTION LIKE A GALAXY OF JAM-PACKED SUNS.

****

STRATEGY 63:

PREFER TO BE A MAN'S MAN. WHEN WE COME AROUND YOU AS PLANETS REVOLVE AROUND THE SUN, DO NOT FEEL EXCITED. BE IN THE LEAD. DO NOT CRAVE FOR US. LET US CRAVE TO BE IN YOUR PRESENCE. CREATE AN AIR OF MYSTERY AND POWER AROUND YOU.

HOUSE RULE 64:

WE PERCEIVE THAT MEN SEEK HAPPINESS AND A CONSTANT SENSE OF MANLINESS AS A THIRSTY CAMEL SEEKS FOR AN OASIS. WE ARE ABLE TO INITIATE WHAT THEY PERCEIVE AS A HAPPY AURA AROUND US AT WILL. THUS WE USE THIS KEY TO "HAPPINESS" TO CONTROL MEN.

****

STRATEGY 64:

REFUSE TO LEAVE THE KEY TO YOUR HAPPINESS OR SELF-ESTEEM IN ANOTHER PERSON'S HANDS. YOU MAY BECOME A MARIONETTE.

HOUSE RULE 65:

IN THE WORKPLACE, WHEN WE LOVE A MAN WHO IS OUR SENIOR, WE CALL HIM BY HIS NAME RATHER THAN BY HIS TITLE. WE ENFORCE A SENSE OF EQUALITY AND FAMILIARITY SO THAT HE CAN BE EXPLOITED TO OUR ADVANTAGE.

****

STRATEGY 65:

STRATEGIC SILENCE AND SUBTLE DISTANCING WILL NORMALLY PUT US BACK IN RESPECTFUL COURSE. SHOULD ANY OF US INSIST ON THE OVER-FAMILIARITY COURSE, STRONGLY ASSERT YOUR POSTURE WITHOUT BEING BRASH; BE BLUNT IF WE ARE PERSISTENTLY UNREPENTANT.

HOUSE RULE 66:

WE DETERMINE IF A MAN HAS A SOFT SPOT FOR US BY LOOKING STRAIGHT INTO HIS EYES; WE WATCH THE DIRECTION OF HIS EYES TO KNOW HIS AREA OF INTEREST. THEN, WE MAY GENTLY OBSERVE THE CONTOUR BELOW HIS BELT FOR SIGNS OF ERECTION.

****

STRATEGY 66:

LIKE A FALCONER AND A SEASONED SPARTAN, OBSERVE OUR EYES. READ-OFF OUR THOUGHTS VIA OUR BODY LANGUAGES – EYE MOVEMENTS, COMPORTMENT, VOICE MODULATION, POSTURE, ETC. MAINTAIN A GURU-LIKE SERENITY.

HOUSE RULE 67:

WE NEVER LET MEN KNOW OUR TRUE STATE OF COMFORT, ESPECIALLY THE SPECIAL FAVOURS WE GET FOR JUST BEING WOMEN.

****

STRATEGY 67:

YOU MUST LEARN TO BE RESERVED IN PETTING US. DO NOT DO OUR EVERY "BIDDING". AFTER ALL, IF YOU DIE, WE WILL COMFORTABLY REPLACE YOU WITH ANOTHER BUFFOON.

HOUSE RULE 68:

AT A CERTAIN AGE AND AS A DISARMING WEAKNESS, WE TEND TO LOVE EASILY AND TO GIVE OUR HEARTS TO CAPABLE MEN WHEN THEY SAY THEY WOULD MARRY US.

****

STRATEGY 68:

DO NOT SAY YOU WANT TO MARRY US IF YOU ARE NOT SURE OF WHAT YOU ARE SAYING. WE MAY BELIEVE YOU. IF YOU THEN TAKE ANOTHER WOMAN TO THE ALTAR, THE CONSEQUENCES MAY BE SO DISASTROUS THAT YOU MAY BE CONSUMED.

HOUSE RULE 69:

AT A YOUNGER BUT EXPERIENCED AGE, WE ARE NOT EUPHORIC WITH MEN WHEN THEY PROPOSE MARRIAGE UNLESS IF WE LOVE THEM VERY DEARLY. WE TEND TO BELIEVE THAT MEN ARE JOKING WITH US AND THAT THEY MAY TAKE ANOTHER LADY TO THE ALTAR. NEVERTHELESS, MANY OF US, UNDER THE PRESSURE OF AGE, CULTURE AND PEERS, FALL LIKE A LOG OF WOOD WHENEVER "MARRIAGE" IS MENTIONED.

****

STRATEGY 69:

BE WISE. IF YOU WANT TO MARRY, THEN DO SO. IF NOT, DO NOT THINK OUR HEARTS WOULD WAIT FOR YOU IN THIS FLOODED WORLD IF YOU DELAY. NEVERTHELESS, BE CAREFUL WITH THE WORD "MARRIAGE". WE MAY RAISE THE HORRIBLE HELL IF YOU DUMP US AFTER BRINGING IN THE WORD "MARRIAGE", ESPECIALLY IF WE FELL FOR IT.

HOUSE RULE 70:

WE MAKE UP OUR FACE AND PUT ON ATTRACTIVE DRESSES AND A FRAGRANT AURA FOR HIS BENEFIT. WE DO THIS TO TRACK HIM DOWN. WE KNOW THAT THEY DO NOT LIKE WOMEN WHO APPEAR STALE AND SAGGED. THEY DO NOT LIKE A WOMAN WHO APPEARS LIKE ONE ABOUT TO DIE.

****

STRATEGY 70:

FORM THE HABIT OF IMAGINING HOW WE WOULD LOOK LIKE IN THE FUTURE. IN OLD AGE, WOULD YOU STILL DIE FOR US? IN THIS HIDE-AND-SEEK GAME OF SEXUAL ORGASM, DO NOT APPEAR LIKE A MORTAL BEING. ASSUME THE POSTURE OF A DEIFIED PHENOMENON THAT WE CANNOT DO WITHOUT.

HOUSE RULE 71:

WE APPLY THE "PERSISTENCE-BREAKS-RESISTANCE" RULE IN STAMPEDING MEN WHO APPEAR INVULNERABLE.

****

STRATEGY 71:

ASIDE FROM THE JOSEPH-LEAVES-CLOTH-AND-FLEES APPROACH TO THIS ISSUE, YOUR ONLY ESCAPE FROM THIS SNARE IS SIMPLE: PERSISTENCE IN RESISTANCE DEVOURS THE PERSISTENCE-BREAKS-RESISTANCE RULE.

HOUSE RULE 72:

WE LIKE POWER. WE LIKE THE POMP AND PAGEANTRY OF POWER. WE LIKE HANGING AROUND PEOPLE WHO MAKE THINGS HAPPEN. THIS IS BECAUSE WE WANT TO BELONG AND BLOSSOM; WE WANT TO LOOK FLASHY, CATCHY AND GOOD.

****

STRATEGY 72:

IF YOU ARE POWERFUL, DO NOT ALLOW US TO TAKE OVER YOUR POWER FROM BEHIND-THE-SCENE. DO NOT ALLOW US TO DETERMINE YOUR DECISIONS. JUST ENJOY US AS WE HANG AROUND YOU – IF YOU WILL. WE ARE ONLY BUTTERFLIES THAT HAVE COME TO SUCK THE NECTAR OF YOUR FLOWER AND HELP YOU POLLINATE IN THE PROCESS. DO NOT LET US SUCK AWAY ALL THE NECTAR...

HOUSE RULE 73:

BY INDUCTION, THE DISCIPLINE OF OUR MAN GETS TO US AND WE MAY TURN OUT TAMED LIKE A HORSE. AND IF WE ARE WELL-TRAINED, DISCIPLINED, GUIDED CONFIDENTLY AND TRUSTFULLY, WE WILL BE GREAT BLESSINGS TO OURSELVES, FAMILIES AND THE SOCIETY.

****

STRATEGY 73:

TAKE UP THE TASK OF INVESTING SPIRITUALLY, EDUCATIONALLY AND FINANCIALLY IN THE FORMATION OF YOUR DAUGHTERS, SISTERS AND WIVES. DO NOT TREAT THEM WITH KID GLOVES. DOING SO WILL BRING YOU UNIMAGINABLE PAIN. PLENTY OF THE PRESENT GIRLS AND WOMEN, WHO ARE RUDE, NAGGING, DEMANDING, LOOSE, SELFISH, BRAGGING, LAZY, TREACHEROUS AND STUPID, ARE THE PRODUCTS OF MEN'S IRRESPONSIBLE BEHAVIOURAL PATTERNS.

HOUSE RULE 74:

WE SECRETLY OR OPENLY CHOKE IN DESPAIR IF OUR MAN HAS ROVING EYES: EYES THAT STARE AT OTHER WOMEN WHILE WE ARE BY HIS SIDE. WE NATURALLY BEGIN TO ACT RIGHT TO KEEP HIM OR WE DUMP HIM FOR ANOTHER MAN.

****

STRATEGY 74:

WE HAVE SOMETHING IN OUR HEADS THAT LIGHT UP WHEN YOU BEGIN TO STARE AT US. IT DOES NOT MATTER IF WE ARE WATCHING YOU OR NOT. WE JUST KNOW YOU ARE LOOKING AT US. THUS, YOUR EYES COMMUNICATE WITH US IN MANY OTHER WAYS THAN YOU MAY EVER KNOW. WE INTERCEPT THIS TELEPATHIC PROCESS WHEN YOU STARE AT OTHER WOMEN ASIDE OURSELVES. LEARN TO COMMUNICATE RESPONSIBLY AND MEASURABLY WITH YOUR EYES.

HOUSE RULE 75:

IN LOVE AND WAR, WE MAINTAIN MILITARY SILENCE. WE DO NOT SPEAK OR CONSORT WITH THE ENEMY. SILENCE IS GOLDEN.

****

STRATEGY 75:

DURING LOVE QUARRELS, YOU MAY NOTICE THAT WE BECOME TACITURN AND SPEAK LESS THAN NECESSARY. IF WE HAD SAID OR DONE ANYTHING BEFORE THEN, WE FEEL A SENSE OF SHAME THAT YOU SEE US AMIDST SUCH WORDS. USE THE MIRROR-EFFECT, THAT IS, DO THE SAME THING TOO. WE WILL BURST FORTH. SEE STRATEGY 1.

HOUSE RULE 76:

DURING A QUARREL, THE BEST OF US DO NOT MAKE A SCENE IN PUBLIC. WE MAY BE BOILING INSIDE OF US BUT WE BAFFLE OUR MAN WITH THE SWEETEST OF SMILES. IN THE EYE OF SMILES COMES THE SWORDS OF STRATAGEMS.

****

STRATEGY 76:

IF YOU NOTICE THIS DURING A QUARREL, READ EVERY MOVE. USE THE MIRROR EFFECT. AS SOON AS WE SEE YOU REFLECTING US, NEGATIVE EMOTIONS WILL BE TRANSFERRED MUCH LIKE THERMODYNAMICS FROM YOU TO US. FRUSTRATED, WE WILL FLARE UP. IF YOU ARE ABLE TO KEEP YOUR COOL WHILE WE LOSE OURS, YOU'RE THE WINNER. WE NEVER FORGET THAT.

HOUSE RULE 77:

DURING A QUARREL, WE NEVER CALL OUR MAN TO DIALOGUE. HE MUST DO THE CALLING. IF HE IS AT FAULT AND STILL LOVES US, HE WILL DEFINITELY CALL US. IF WE DO NOT GET A CALL AFTER A CONSIDERABLE WHILE, HE IS A WICKED FOOL WHO DOES NOT DESERVE US. IF HE CALLS, WE WILL NEVER PICK THE FIRST CALL. IF HE CALLS AGAIN, WE WILL FRAME A MEETING OR ANY OTHER SITUATION THAT WOULD MAKE US VERY BRIEF ON PHONE AND GIVE US THE ADVANTAGE TO RUSH HIM OFF THE PHONE. WE MAY SUGGEST TO HIM A SPECIFIC TIME OF OUR CHOICE FOR THE CONVERSATION—ALL THESE, WITH THE SWEETEST OF VOICE. IF HE IS A MINUTE LATE FROM THE SPECIFIED TIME, THE CYCLE BEGINS AGAIN. WE MAY OR MAY NOT GO THIS FAR. IT ALL DEPENDS ON THE CONSEQUENCES WE EXPECT.

STRATEGY 77:

DURING A QUARREL, WHOEVER CALLS FIRST, LOSES GROUND. THE OTHER PERSON GETS THE UPPER HAND. HOWEVER, IF YOU KNOW YOU ARE AT FAULT, PLEASE DO THE CALLING. WE GET A SHATTERED IMAGE OF YOU IF YOU DO NOT DO THIS. SENIOR STRATEGISTS WOULD DELIBERATELY PREFER TO GO TO WHERE THEY KNOW THEY WOULD FIND THEIR WOMAN (PREFERABLY HER CHURCH OR MOSQUE) AND PRETEND TO BE BUSY AND HAPPY WITH OTHER PEOPLE WHEN THEY KNOW SHE HAD SEEN THEM. THEN WHEN THEY SENSE THAT THEIR CHARMING AND FRAGRANT PRESENCE HAS THWARTED THE ANGER IN HER, THEY WOULD WALK OVER TO HER AND MESMERIZE HER WITH THEIR EYES AND TONGUE BEFORE SHE MAKES ANY COUNTER-MOVE. PHYSICAL PRESENCE IS TOO MUCH OF A DISTRACTION FOR US. THIS IS WHY LOVERS WHO ARE CLASSMATES HARDLY EVER SEPARATE.

HOUSE RULE 78:

DURING A QUARREL, WE EMPLOY THE WEAPON OF TENTERHOOKS. WE KEEP OUR MAN WAITING SOMEHOW. WAITING BUILDS ANXIETY AND GREAT SUSPENSE. AND IF WE DO NOT WANT HIM ANY LONGER, WE BREAK UP WITH HIM BEFORE HE BREAKS UP WITH US. WHOEVER DICTATES THE BREAK-UP FIRST IS THE LAST MAN STANDING.

****

STRATEGY 78:

NEVER ALLOW A WOMAN TO BREAK UP A RELATIONSHIP FIRST. IF SHE DOES, CALL HER AGAIN AND APOLOGIZE. THEN BREAK UP WITH HER AFTER A WHILE. WHOEVER DICTATES THE BREAK-UP LAST IS ALSO THE LAST MAN STANDING....

OF COURSE, YOU DO THIS ONLY WHEN YOU DO NOT WANT HER AGAIN. THERE ARE MANY OF US OUT THERE WAITING TO HAVE YOU AFTER ALL.

HOUSE RULE 79:

WHEN WE SENSE THAT WE ARE INDISPENSABLE TO A MAN, HE IS AT OUR MERCY.

****

STRATEGY 79:

IF YOU WANT TO BE IN CHARGE OF A RELATIONSHIP, YOU MUST FROM ITS INCEPTION, BE DISPOSED TO LOSE YOUR WOMAN IF NECESSARY. NO MATTER HOW MUCH YOU LOVE US, TREAT US AS DISPENSABLE. YOU ARE BETTER OFF THAT WAY.

HOUSE RULE 80:

SOME OF US LIKE TO DRIVE MEN TO WORK FOR THEM LIKE A BULLDOZER. IF THEIR VICTIMS DIE IN THE PROCESS, THEY MOURN THEM. BUT, THEN, LIFE CONTINUES.

****

STRATEGY 80:

YOU ARE NOT IRREPLACEABLE. NOBODY REALLY IS. THEREFORE, WATCH THE PRESSURES YOU TAKE FROM US. THE WEALTH OF A DEAD MAN DOES NOT GO WITH HIM TO THE GRAVE.

HOUSE RULE 81:

THE BEST OF US CONTROL MEN WITHOUT LETTING THE MEN KNOW OF IT. WE MAKE THEM FEEL THEY ARE IN CHARGE WHEN THE REVERSE IS ACTUALLY THE CASE.

****

STRATEGY 81:

GIVE A DOG A BONE AND SEE HOW IT TAKES IT. GIVE US LITTLE POWER AND SEE WHAT IT DOES TO US. WHAT WE BECOME AFTER THAT SHOWS OUR TRUE INTENTIONS.

HOUSE RULE 82:

AS INDIVIDUAL QUEENS, WE MAINTAIN A NETWORK OF FRIENDS TO WHOM WE MAKE DISTRESS CALLS IN TIMES OF TROUBLES AND DURING TIMES OF STRATEGIC NEEDS. YET THE ADVICE WE RECEIVE HARDLY EVER BUILDS BUT QUITE OFTEN BREAKS RELATIONSHIPS.

****

STRATEGY 82:

YOU MUST MAKE SURE YOUR WOMAN DOES NOT PERSISTENTLY DEPEND ON HER FRIENDS IN TIMES OF TROUBLES. YOU ARE IN TROUBLE IF YOU ALLOW THIS. TRAIN HER TO RESIST THAT SHEEP INSTINCT.

HOUSE RULE 83:

OUR SUCCESS WITH MEN DEPENDS ON THE IMPRESSION THEY HAVE ABOUT US. THUS, WE JEALOUSLY GUARD OUR ANTECEDENTS/ PAST.

****

STRATEGY 83:

VANITY IS ABROAD. KNOW OUR TRUE CIRCUMSTANCES. KNOW OUR PAST. KNOW WHAT YOU ARE IN LOVE WITH!

HOUSE RULE 84:

LIKE THE UNTRAINED EYE, THE EYES OF MEN PICK ON THE APPEARANCES OF WOMEN. THUS, WE ARE MERCILESSLY METICULOUS WITH OUR AESTHETIC DESIGNS.

****

STRATEGY 84:

ALL THAT GLITTERS IS NOT GOLD. DO NOT BE DECEIVED BY APPEARANCES. SOME OF US ARE HORRIBLE UNDER THOSE CLOTHES.

HOUSE RULE 85:

QUITE OFTEN, THE BEAUTIFUL ONES AMONG US BECOME SO THROUGH THE EFFORTS OF MANY MEN. THE BEAUTIFUL CLOTHS, THE SOFT SUCCULENT SKIN, THE RESPLENDENT HAIR-DO AND THE CATWALK – INDUCED STILETTOED SHOES IN ONE GIRL MIGHT ALL COME CONCURRENTLY THROUGH THE EFFORTS OF MANY MEN.

****

STRATEGY 85:

WHEN YOU DISCOVER YOU LOVE A BEAUTIFUL GIRL, BEWARE OF DOGS. THERE MAY BE OTHER TERRITORIAL MASTERS. BE SURE YOU ARE CAPABLE....

HOUSE RULE 86:

WHEN WE ARE WRONGED, WE MAY FORGIVE BUT WE RARELY FORGET. OFTEN TIMES, WE ARE LIKELY TO AVENGE OURSELVES OF THOSE WRONGS.

****

STRATEGY 86:

WHEN YOU WRONG ANY OF US AND WE COME TO THE ART OF FORGIVENESS, DEFUSE THE REINFORCEMENT OF PAST WRONGS BY THE SHOW OF YOUR LOVE.

HOUSE RULE 87:

WE FUNCTION BY THE SHEEP-INSTINCT. WE HARDLY EVER MOVE ALONE, WE WOULD BE LIABLE TO FALL FOR MEN IF SO.

* * * * * * * *

STRATEGY 87:

CONFRONT THE SHEEP CIRCLE. BE SURE YOU HAVE THE PARAPHERNALIA TO DO THIS. ENCIRCLE US AND ISOLATE THE TARGET.

HOUSE RULE 88:

IN DESPERATE MOMENTS, WE SET FALSE PRECEDENCE, I.E. WE APOLOGIZE FOR NOT CALLING ON YOU AS IF YOU HAD ASKED US TO DO SO, WHEN IN ACTUAL FACT, YOU DID NO SUCH THING.

****

STRATEGY 88:

IGNORE THE ATTEMPT TO ACT ON OUR SUBSTITUTED PRECEDENCE, WHICH ACTION IS OUR INTENDED DESIRE.

HOUSE RULE 89:

LIKE GOLD DIGGERS, WE GO TO THE MEN WHO HAVE THE KEY TO THE GOLDMINES WE SEEK. THE GOLDMINES MAY BE GRADES, MONEY, FAME, ETC. NO QUEEN WANTS TO SUFFER.

****

STRATEGY 89:

WHEN WE FLOOD YOU, MAKE SURE YOU KNOW THE REASONS WHY WE DO THIS. USE THE KEY AS BAIT TO DRAW AND CONFINE US AS YOU WILL.

HOUSE RULE 90:

QUEENS BEHAVE LIKE QUEENS. WE ARE MUCH ALIKE. THUS, WE INSTANTLY BECOME PREDICTABLE AND VULNERABLE TO THE MEN WHO BREAK THROUGH OUR COMMON CODES.

****

STRATEGY 90:

YOU MUST STRIVE TO DECIPHER OUR HIEROGLYPHICS AND CUNEIFORM. IF YOU SUCCEED, OUR WORLD BECOMES YOUR OYSTER. WE DREAD YOU IF YOU ARE A MASTER.

HOUSE RULE 91:

AS THE TORTOISE GOING ABOUT HIS BUSINESS, THE ABLEST QUEENS UNDERSTAND THAT THEIR EFFICIENCY AND EFFECTIVENESS MUST PASS THROUGH THE CRUCIBLE OF CAREFUL PLANNING.

****

STRATEGY 91:

USE THE MIRROR EFFECT HERE. ALSO PLAN TO THE VERY END. FURTHERMORE, ALWAYS HAVE ALTERNATIVE PLANS IN YOUR KITTY SHOULD SURPRISES SPRING FORTH.

HOUSE RULE 92:

ALTHOUGH FREE THINGS ARE NOT VALUED, WE KNOW THAT FREE THINGS ARE DANGEROUS. NEVERTHELESS, WE ACCEPT FREE THINGS FROM FOOLISH MEN.

****

STRATEGY 92:

YOU SHOULD HAVE A REASON FOR ANYTHING YOU GIVE A WOMAN. IN CERTAIN CASES, YOU MUST MAKE US KNOW, *AB INITIO,* WHY YOU GIVE US A GIFT OR ELSE YOU WILL HURT YOURSELF AT THE TIME OF RECKONING.

HOUSE RULE 93:

WE ARE MORE COMFORTABLE AND SECURE WITH HAVING FORMER QUEENS (NOW MARRIED QUEENS) AS TECHNICAL ADVISERS, ONLY BECAUSE THEY ARE LESS LIKELY TO BE OUR COMPETITORS.

****

STRATEGY 93:

MONITOR EVERY MARRIED QUEEN THAT IS VERY FRIENDLY TO YOUR WOMAN. IN FORESTALLING ALL INFLUENCE OF THESE MARRIED QUEENS, REMOVE THE CHAFF AMONG THEM FROM THE MAIZE.

HOUSE RULE 94:

NO QUEEN STEPS INTO THE SHOES OF ANOTHER QUEEN. EVERY QUEEN DEFINES HER POSITION AND CHOOSES TO BE ACCEPTED THAT WAY.

****

STRATEGY 94:

WHEN THE MATTER IS INCONSEQUENTIAL, ALLOW HER TO HAVE A FIELD DAY. BUT AT MOMENTS OF GRAVE IMPORTANCE, THE LAST BUCK SHOULD LAND ON YOUR DESK.

HOUSE RULE 95:

EVERY QUEEN, NO MATTER HOW UGLY AND NASTY IN CHARACTER AND PHYSIOGNOMY, ALWAYS FRAMES THE AURA OF PERFECTION AND BEING IN HIGH DEMAND. WE MAKE MEN BELIEVE THAT EVERY OTHER MAN IS AFTER US, EVEN WHEN THE REVERSE IS THE CASE.

****

STRATEGY 95:
SEE STRATEGY 79.

HOUSE RULE 96:

JUST LIKE THE CHAMELEON, WE TAKE THE COLOUR OF OUR ENVIRONMENT. WE ASSUME THE SHAPE OF OUR HOST. WE THRIVE IN FORMLESS QUEENSHIP.

****

STRATEGY 96:

EITHER USE THE MIRROR EFFECT TO ASSUME SHAPELESSNESS *JUST LIKE THE CHAMELEON AND TAKE THE COLOUR OF OUR ENVIRONMENT* OR ASSUME VARIED COLOURS WITHOUT BEING IDENTIFIED WITH ANY. LEAD AND PACE.

HOUSE RULE 97:

ALL MOTHER-QUEENS MAKE THEIR PAWN-DAUGHTERS INTO QUEENS. LIKE THE VAMPIRE, MOTHER-QUEENS BITE THE VIRUS INTO THEIR DAUGHTERS. WE ARE QUEENS, WE KNOW THE RULES OF ENGAGEMENT.

****

STRATEGY 97:

PREPARE TO BE A FATHER-KING. PREPARE TO BITE THE VIRUS OF STRATEGIES INTO YOUR PAWN-SONS. PREPARE TO MAKE THEM INTO KINGS. PREPARE THEM WITH THE EQUITABLE ARMAMENTS. PREPARE THEM FOR PRE-EMPTIVE STRIKES.

HOUSE RULE 98:

DURING PREGNANCY, SOME OF US, ESPECIALLY THOSE WHO CLAIM SOPHISTICATION, MAKE OUR MEN DO THE DOMESTIC CHORES. AND WE WATCH AND WE WEIGH HOW OUR MEN BUCKLE UNDER OUR INFLUENCE WHICH MAY CONTINUE ONLY BY THE LAW OF INERTIA OR REFLEX ACTION EVEN AFTER THE GESTATION OF ONLY NINE MONTHS.

****

STRATEGY 98:

DURING THE GESTATION OF YOUR WOMAN, *SELECTIVELY* GIVE IN TO HER DEMANDS. RETURN TO THE PRE-GESTATION POSTURE AFTER DELIVERY.

HOUSE RULE 99:

WE EASILY INTERPRET THE UNATTACHED CIVILITY OF MEN AS SECRET AFFECTION AND DESIRE FOR INTIMATE RELATIONSHIP WITH US.

****

STRATEGY 99:

DECLARE FROM THE ONSET THAT THERE ARE NO STRINGS ATTACHED TO YOUR ACTIONS, EVEN IF THERE ARE. WE WOULD LIKE YOU FOR THIS CULTURED MANOEUVRE.

HOUSE RULE 100:

WHEN WE WANT TO BREAK OR CATCH A MAN, WE LIKE TO IDENTIFY WITH HIS LIKES AND DISLIKES. SHOULD HE BE STUBBORN OR SLOW TO IDENTIFY US, WE PERSIST WITH PUBLISHING OUR VERISIMILITUDE OF HIS NATURE IN HIS VERY GAZE, FOR WE KNOW THAT MEN LIKE THEIR REPLICAS.

****

STRATEGY 100:

BIRDS OF A FEATHER FLOCK TOGETHER. KNOW THE SNAKE FROM THE GREEN GRASS. UNDERSTAND THE WOLF AND THE SHEEP. CONSIDER THE GUINEA FOWL AND THE FOWL. SPOT THE DIFFERENCE AND BE WISE.

FIRST SENSE:

EVEN WHEN THEY DO, THE GREATEST OF MEN DO NOT APPEAR TO PURSUE WOMEN. FOR THIS, WOMEN PURSUE THEM

SECOND SENSE:

REMEMBER THE FIRST MAN, ADAM OR ADAMU, HE DISASTROUSLY SUBMITTED TO EVE AND CHANGED THE COURSE OF THE HUMAN RACE.

THIRD SENSE:

TAKE NOTE OF THE WISEST MAN, SOLOMON OR SULEIMAN, HE HAD HUNDREDS OF WOMEN AND EVEN KNEW SOME HOUSE RULES, YET HE FAILED BECAUSE OF THE NON-IMPLEMENTATION OF STRATEGIES.

FOURTH SENSE:

CONSIDER THE STRONGEST OF MEN, SAMSON, HE FELL FOR THE EPHEMERAL BEAUTY THAT IS DELILAH AND PAID WITH HIS SIGHT AND MIGHTY STRENGTH.

FIFTH SENSE:

IF HORMONES AND NERVE SENSATIONS ARE REMOVED FROM THE CHEMISTRY OF LOVE OR LOVE MAKING, WHAT WILL REMAIN IS AN EMPTY RUBBING OF MUCOUS FLESH AND A REALIZATION THAT MANKIND HAS BEEN UNDER A BLISSFUL ILLUSION WHICH ONLY SOME WOMEN ARE HALF-AWAKE FROM. ACTUALLY, THE ICING OF EMOTIONS IS NEEDED TO MAKE THE JOB OF PROCREATION WORTH THE WHILE. THANK GOD FOR THIS.

SIXTH SENSE:

IN CONCLUSION, THE MOST RECURRING DIFFERENCE BETWEEN THE WISE AND THE FOOLISH IS THE USE OR NON-USE OF FORESIGHT....

POSTSCRIPT

In the *Communist Manifesto*, Karl Marx in collaboration with Friedrich Engels said that the "history of all hitherto existing society is the history of class struggle". In life, there are different types of classes of which men and women are examples, even though Marx did not concern himself with this fact. Men and women have been struggling against each other for survival, ultimately and no ignorance, unfortunately, can exempt any man or woman from the reality of the struggle. Knowledge of the war is only a first step in assuming a responsible and responsive posture towards the battle. To acknowledge, identify, isolate and appreciate the rules of engagement in the ongoing encounter is the second step in the call to stand up and ameliorate the damaging fruits of this war. *The Secret Principles of Female Powers* is a humble contribution to these acknowledgements.

Men are generally timid, stupid, and unskilled in the dynamics and art of engaging the opposite sex. This is largely because from boyhood their fathers do not inculcate in them the knowledge on how to relate with girls and women, except to be brutish and vulgar. Right from the kitchen, the girl learns from the mother or significant women (relational mentors) the nitty-gritty of handling men. Thus, girls and women are generally wiser, more mature and skilful than boys and men, who are, chronologically speaking, their age-mates. This cannot be gainsaid, as we only need to see how younger girls and women masterfully contain older boys and men. In order to help reduce the level of idiocy constantly published by the males, *The Secret Principles of Female Powers* was born.

In Yetunde Arebi's "The Human Angle" column of the *Vanguard* of Thursday, March 16, 2000, a man cried distressingly for solution when he said, "you women are very crafty and only God can deliver us from your hands. If a woman is determined to have a man, only God can save him from her. A woman is shrouded in secrecy and deceit which is why their secret place is located inside their body". To such distressed men, *The Secret Principles of Female Powers* has laid open the feminine chamber of secrecy; thus letting men know that God is always ready to help, but man has the job of being God's partner by doing his part, namely learning from life. Ignorance, the Holy Book says, is the reason God's people perish (Hosea 4:6). God did not come from heaven to teach the females; He will not come down to teach the males. Man must stop being sluggard. On account of not disposing oneself to knowledge one fails to have refined methods of relating with the female; this lack of refinement is the mother of rape, wife beating, murder, female-child pregnancy, and other forms of violence against women. With a deep understanding of how the female functions via the principles they follow without necessarily being physically violent, men can also face the demands of relating with the opposite sex by way of using the tools, the strategies to the House Rules in the psychological war of women against men.

A PARTING POEM

Girls in skirts that open the way

Walk past us in a sexy way

Try all we can to look away

What goes around

Sure comes around.

These, Lord Byron saw years past

And Lord Jeff did hope to fast

But Don Juan knows how to cast

A wandering look

A tempting hook

Leila's legs on platform shoes,

Pampered trunks in skimpy hugs,

Woven hair of green? Brown? Blue?

Provocative laps....
Colorizing lips....

Big backsides and parting laps,
Julia's orbs in slipping bras,
Nude navels in flashy cars,
Tempestuous gums....
Calculative smacks....

Heidée's fingers browse around,
Seductive laughter coos aloud,
Sultana's fragrance spreads about,
Magnetic breasts....
Hypnotic hips....

The Don must have closed his eyes
Hoping to just throw his dice
But he tumbles off the ice
Snooping around
Wondering aloud

Cool hot heads in expensive airs,
Great coy moves to pummel the way,
Star-snubbing nails poking won heads,
Artificial frowns....
Superficial tears....

Soft slippery baits in feverish grasps,
Strange fickle minds slipping from grabs,
Full catwalks eliciting gasps,
Tantalizing tongues....
Petrifying pecks....

Full luscious lips which kiss wiz kids,
Long oily nails which trace chained cheeks,
Strong lustful eyes on weak gawping freaks,
Titillating toes....
Mesmerizing tones....

Try all we can to look away,
Only end up with eyes at bay,
Oh Universe, help keep at bay:

Romantic eyes....

Suggestive smiles....

(First written at Eni Njoku Hall, Nsukka, 2002, reedited January 15, 2019).

SUGGESTIONS FOR FURTHER READING

Allen, J. & Shelden, D., eds. *Picking on Men Again.* London: Arrow Books, 1986.

Bhaktipada, S. *The Joy of No Sex.* West Virginia: New Vrindaban, 1988.

Chinweizu. *The Anatomy of Female Powers.* Lagos: Abelard – Shuman, 1990.

De Beauvoir, S. *Second Sex.* New York: Vintage Books, 1989.

Deutsch, H. *The Psychology of Women.* Vol. II. New York: Bantam, 1973.

Esther, V. *The Manipulated Man.* London: Abelard – Shuman, 1972.

Friedman, B. *The Feminine Mystique.* Harmondsworth: Penguin, 1965.

Greene, R. *The 48 Laws of Power.* New York: Penguin Books, 1998.

Hammond, M. M. *Finding the Right Woman for You: One Woman's Advice to Men.* Oregon: Harvest House Publishers, 1973.

Steel, D. *The Long Road Home.* London: BCA, 1998.

Trobisch, W. *Living with Unfulfilled Desires.* Kehl/ Rhein: Editions Trobisch, 1980.